The

Red Leaves

of

Night

Also by David St. John

Hush (1976)
The Shore (1980)
No Heaven (1985)
Terraces of Rain: An Italian Sketchbook (1991)
Study for the World's Body (1994)

LIMITED EDITIONS
For Lerida (1973)
The Olive Grove (1980)
A Folio of Lost Worlds (1981)
The Man in the Yellow Gloves (1985)
The Orange Piano (1987)

The
Red Leaves
of Night

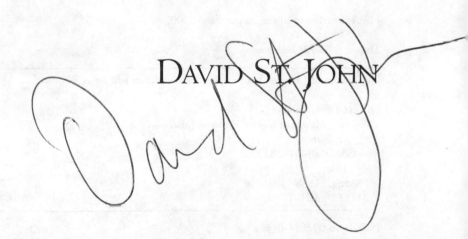

DAVID ST. JOHN

HarperPerennial
A Division of HarperCollinsPublishers

First HarperPerennial edition published 2000.

Designed by Elina D. Nudelman

The Library of Congress has catalogued the hardcover edition as follows:

St. John, David, 1949–
    The red leaves of night / David St. John. — 1st ed.
        p.   cm
    ISBN 0-06-019283-6
    I. Title
PS3569.A4536R4   1999
811'.54—dc21   98-7772

ISBN 0-06-093016-0 (pbk.)

00 01 02 03 04 ❖/RRD 10 9 8 7 6 5 4 3 2 1

for Molly

Contents

Acknowledgments

American Literary Review: "Naked"; "The Pianist"; "Music"; "Apple Orchard"; "Levels of Retreat"

American Poetry Review: "Nocturnes & Aubades"; "Patience"; "Ravenesque"; "An Invitation"; "A Naked Truth"; "Not a Man"; "Waves"

Antaeus: "The Figure *You*"; "Night"

Colorado Review: "Troubadour"; "Fleurs Mystiques"

Denver Quarterly: "The Unsayable, the Unknowable & You"; "Stories"; "Prayer to Ondine"; "Solitude"

The Harvard Review: "Beeches"

The Kenyon Review: "Portrait"; "Accomplishment"; "The Bowl"; "What He Said"; "Adam"

The Paris Review: "The Park"

Poetry: "Rhapsody"

Volt: "Memphis"

Western Humanities Review: "Water Serpents"; "Water Serpents (II)"

The Yale Review: "Chevalier d'Or"

"In the Sulphur Garden" appeared in *The Writing Path*, edited by Michael Pettitt (University of Iowa Press, 1995).

"Troubadour" appeared in *The 1998 Pushcart Prize XXII*, edited by Bill Henderson (Pushcart Press, 1998).

Thanks to the Getty Research Institute for the History of Art and the Humanities for their Visiting Scholar residency.

Nocturnes & Aubades

The Figure *You*

The figure *you*
Remains the speculative whip of my aesthetic

As in the latest chapter I've been writing
Called "The Erotics of the Disembodied Self"

Although I suppose the figure
You still suppose yourself to be is nevertheless

& upon reflection nothing more than the presence
Of someone else's moon-stunned body

Held quietly against your own just like the air
Or any other absence by which we learn to mark

The passing of yet another impossibly forgiven
& long-punishable night

Nocturnes & Aubades

I. ZONES

It was in the night's minute disturbances
(You said) that you'd discovered the exquisite

Composition of desire, in those beautiful

Zones of the darkened sundial held out
Just before the sculling of the day.

Yet as you slowly burned the gathered cloth

Of every nerve we'd ever sewn, I also awoke
As the apparition you'd believed

I was; & we rose at last—that last morning—

Within the lit pearl, its prelude to sunlight,
Those long black grasses still lifting

Their delicate heads to the breeze . . . still

Resolute in the old desires & thirsts. The way tonight,
Sitting alone in this distant hotel, I lift another

Shattered glass of stars to you. . . .

II. THE PEAR

Tears are like luck, they come last
To those who most deserve them—

The powdered china of your body,
Its porcelain sheen in the streaked pulse

Of scalding moonlight. Smoke rises,
Pumping above the city's black towers;

Yet as the tea of the night's ghosts
Seeps into your limp hands, already

The fortune told by its leaves begins
Honing itself into a tiny locket

Shaped not like a heart but like that one
Miniature pear we saw on the Ponte Vecchio,

Carved of marble, the top of a thumb:
White as fear: petrified pearl—

Fallen, stunted tear of the goddess.

III. THE VILLAGE

There are so many pianos still left

In the fields of the village
Where you insist that we continue

To live, so many pianos

Though only a few have remained faithful
To the serious chords of the wind.

For example, the camel-colored Steinway

Beneath the ancient arbor of lavender wisteria
& drooping bougainvillaea has barely

A dozen keys left working, their thin felt

Hammers long grown as soggy as dawn mist,
Soft as the pillowing fog.

Still, you say, who cares? as you turn from me,

Stepping calmly onto the narrow stone terrace
Overlooking these perpetual fields—

Just as every young woman in this

Village stands each morning, every one of them,
& exactly at this moment of the day, satisfied by

The first ripple of light as it sketches

The body's languid harmony. If I am lucky, I know
I will live forever in this ancient, lost village

Of pianos & a late pagan petulance.

IV. ROMAN VENUE

Tonight I believe the architecture
Of the moon requires no argument; it exists
As a melody exists, overheard by a man out walking

At dawn, a man who can imagine its notes scored
Across the sky, who knows the songs
Escaping the latticed windows above him are like

Delicate ladders ascending to a perfect room, no,
A sequence of rooms, each more perfect
Than the one before . . . each more luminous & whole,

Like the arc of a melody framing the horizon of the night,
Where a last frail note hangs, ripe as a vowel—utterly
Calm, utterly white—& as that man climbs into

This empty portico of the suspended moment
He hears nothing but those long, struck chords of
Silence, & the round door dilates, sexual as the waking mind.

V. A Pact

It is not so hard to love a ghost

As some friends might try to tell you;
People do it for years, I hear, with almost

Nobody noticing. One night, I held a silver gun

To my head, just to imagine myself as the ghost-to-be,
Nobody special, just myself only—you know, so pale

& thin you could see right through me, just

Like a thistle. Figure it out: I'm here, but I'm not.
That's what happened to me the evening you said

You'd be happier if I were dead. So, I said

I'm sorry; I'm here. I'm not. Sooner or later, a man simply
Burns the toast. It's not so hard to leave you

As it seems, old ghost.

VI. BLESSINGS

Everything broke into absence, as if
That were a good thing. First, the weather
Stood up from its bed & quietly quivered,

& then you quivered. The windows awoke, all caked
With speckles of frost, opaque as those screens
Of carved pearl in your mother's bedroom.

The night is over. The day is finally uncurling
Like a maidenhair fern lifted by the damp finger
Of the light, & everything is broken.

Everything in me is broken. Your absence,
Carving its face on every single window of the cold,
Where you've left me, as if that were a good thing,

The way you act. As if that were a good thing,
The way your absence has carved me into a pale mask:
My eyelids, shaved flakes of mother-of-pearl.

VII. Lost Lives

What were the factors of her songs?
Less particular than cloud, of course,

But roughly the same *contrescarpe* of sky.
We sat through a whole evening of blue stones

Arranged at first randomly, then sadly, into
Letters spelling the names of old lovers—

& Ondine, she'd used up all of the stones before
I could begin even the first letter of a single

Name. Some nights are like that, I know, filled by
Streaks of sweat on satin sheets, & wine stains

Mapping every faint, implausible dream.

VIII. Cosmos

I have a television in my old limousine,
The one I will sell next week to my friend Xavier.
For over a year now it's stood in my driveway

Since you were the only one I would let drive it.
Last summer, finally, I hooked up my new video player
To its small TV & since then that's where I go

To watch all of my fading tapes of you—
The one of you doing the hully-gully with Nico at the ashram;
Or bathing for hours in that old tin tub high in the Sierras;

& my favorite, where you walk the frozen streets of Philadelphia
Humming random passages of *Madama Butterfly*. I still miss
The back of your head, too, especially the soft, babylike skin

At the nape of your neck, freckled lightly, like the grain
Of some unearthly wood; & I still miss the skinny band
Of platinum hair that touched that skin, & the way

Its cool silver shone below the stiff edge of your
Chauffeur's cap. I know the neighbors think it's strange the way
I sit here going nowhere, the TV on, the tapes all showing

The endless road ahead, & the stilled, impassable night.

IX. LOVING ROMY SCHNEIDER

It was a line from Schiller
Set by Schumann, I think, that she wrote
In the flyleaf of the small photo album
Filled entirely with postcards of nudes—
Some male & some female—but each

More miraculous (not to mention immortal)
In their marble flesh than we, who, of course,
Exhausted & sleepless & spent, collapsed into
That coma of the loved & wounded, or vice versa.
Of all the nudes, I preferred the Rodins,

Those postcards being a little grainy & indistinct,
Sort of how I think of myself in the early morning.
Then I put the Schumann on my ancient, almost antique
Turntable, & the whole of my fate revolves slowly
Into some kind of brutal focus, at last.

X. Another Stranger

A lot of life is simply furniture,
Isn't it? I mean, we stumble into & around

Almost all of the most important things
That happen to us. All of this philosophical

Urgency telling us to direct our energies—
Moral & artistic, etc.—is beyond silly, since those

Pretensions evaporate the moment our glazed eyes
Begin to clear. Besides, I liked the surprise

Of bumping into you accidentally like that, the wine
Shivering in your hand, the night sky listing, rapt

With whispers, a whole future assembling, the abandoned
Room kissed awake by the steps of a stranger.

XI. VESPA VESTALS

In the garden of the Virgins, that is,
The garden of the House of the Vestals

(Your sweater draped across your shoulders
As the narrow chill of the evening

Began to ribbon the Forum), you walked
With your head down, silent, a little amused,

But silent. Whatever else exists
In the daily mystery of service & denial

I doubt humor plays much of a part;
Yet there you were, at the ancient threshold

Of the ruins of the House—thinking
Whatever it was that you were thinking—the lush,

Complicated vines of spring already obscuring
The bare stones of the rooms around us.

Yet for some, I know, a little humor is all
That allows our frail dignity to fall

So far from silence, & service, or fortune . . .
To begin yet again as if, each time one loved,

One loved as a virgin, helplessly, if faithlessly—
Until the life that was once long ago imagined

Begins laughing again, silently, in the ruins.

XII. STONE SHADOWS

For an entire year she dressed in all the shades
Of ash—the gray of old paper; the deeper,
Almost auburn ash of pencil boxes; the dark, nearly

Black marl of oak beds pulled from burning houses.
That year, even her hair itself was woven
With an ashen white, just single threads here & there,

Yet the effect at last was of a woman
Constructed entirely of evening shadows . . . walking
Toward you out of an antique ink-&-pearl snapshot.

Still, it was exactly the kind of sadness
I could understand, & even love; & so, I spent hours
Walking the back streets of Trastevere looking in the most

Forbidding & derelict shops for some element of ash
She'd never seen before. It may seem odd to you, now,
But this was the single ambition of my life. Finally,

I had to give it up; I'd failed. She knew them all. So,
To celebrate our few months together, I gave her
Before we parted one night a necklace with a huge fake

Ruby. She slipped it immediately over her head, & its knuckle
Of red glass caught the light reflecting off the thin candles
Rising by the bed. On her naked breasts it looked exactly

Like an unworldly, burgundy coal.

XIII. SICILIAN SMOKE

I know now that I believe only
In what is impossible & without value
In the everyday world, the way the sketched scarlet
Smoke at sunset in Selinunte meant nothing
To the ancient Classicist bent above his shards,

Though of course he had his reasons. I know now
That I believe only in the soft breath of hair, so
Blond it is almost white, so black it falls like night,
So amber & red it is a jewel. Only in that breath
That casts the early light each morning as you lift an arm

To your face & cover your eyes, the abandon of such a refusal,
The daily waste of spoiled light spilling along the red stones
Of the terrace. Such a desire to remain in the sea of solitary
Dream, where no one who ever goes can return with even one
Suitable, memorable, or recognizable belief. I know now

This is the gift your body brings, each morning; the relief.

XIV. From the Lake

In those days you were still in love
With Dante, & Dante, I think, was almost in love
With you. You'd drive him to your parents' place
Up at the lake, & after you'd fucked him stupid
You'd leave him asleep in your girlhood bed, walk
Downstairs & out onto the veranda, sitting naked
In the moonlight in one of the old Adirondack chairs,
The wild cat from the woods suddenly arriving
To curl on your warm stomach, & you'd pick up
The phone, & call me, leaving me a message, a message
So desperate that every time, as you were speaking, I could
Barely keep myself from lifting the receiver
From its cold cradle, though even if I had I suppose
You'd have simply continued to speak on to no one. That is,
To me alone, always me, alone.

XV. ABOVE FLORENCE

Late, & the shades gather their little packets
Of belongings as the milky shallows of the evening
Roll up the awnings of the sky. We shift

The sense of things a little, easily rustling
A few clothes as they're thrown across the bed or floor,

& a few trumpet notes float up out of the black mesh . . .
Cooling once again all of the fires we watch together, like this,
As they arise, so slowly, from the arachnine city below.

XVI. A Traveller

I have travelled so far to remember
Nothing of my former life, though perhaps that is
Truly best. I've left everything I've ever known

To come here, to stand in the shape of your shadow.
If you know little else, know that the distance from the moon
To your bed is only seconds in the mind, the blaze of an idea

Like the flicker of fireflies, hundreds upon hundreds, wave
After wave, the rippling of illuminations along a face—
Like that silent movie in which the heroine, as clear

As black-&-white, travels at last to the end of her solitude.
Just so we're not confused about this kind of thing, don't forget
That it's I who am like her, or she like me, or I like you—

Whose insistence upon distance I've been given to despise.

XVII. SUMMER ABSTRACT

The little yellow vowels rose out of our mouths
Like knots in the river current, like sudden blotches

On a sketchbook. Sallow, the words. Octaves
Of orange light finger, today, the sequence of postures

You perform: turn, wake, & rise. There is nothing
Left for us to deflect in what we say. Instead, we

Pull ourselves up by the customary braids of day,
Though your hair seemed more urgent this morning, its

Usual halo not so fixed & obtrusive. You know, if
You breathe a little more slowly, even your hair (so

Translucent & red lately) will wave in the near
Twilight just like a flag, I mean a real one; I mean

A real silken nervous flag.

XVIII. Nocturne Melting to Aubade

Such a cargo of the self seems so
Inhuman in the dark, the leather straps & heavily

Feathered masks. Still, the one of the nightingale

Still makes me, I confess, start awake the moment
I feel its downy cheek against my thigh. Such

A cargo of the broken self, such wreckage

We bring to sail beneath the stars. In
Another time, another volume of indiscretions,

We might have had—on our side, Iseult—

The whole history of tragedy, the cliffs slowly
Whitening in the dawn ahead. Now, I suppose,

There is little left to ask, little that remains—

Only the small cocoon made by the waves washing
Their prayers over the slow, whispering sheets

Of the final nocturne, even as it ravels to the day.

Is there any landscape more forbidding, more
Abstract? Is there any song no less, no more, a lie?

We sail, like rain, against the sky.

In the Sulphur Garden

Every passage exists simply as a fragment
Of our future remains & therefore
She said to me as each fragrant
Intersection of the wind & leaves bristled
Through the smoke of the cloud-cloaked afternoon

Therefore every body she said
For example my own may seem a bit distorted
By such an unusual if requisite
Perfection & certainly one can hold for
Only an instant in the imagination the very

Idea of the imagination turning so
Suddenly to flesh don't you
Agree & as she paused before the marble genitals
Of the ancient rain-stained Apollo
She reached out instinctively to take a firm hold of

The lancelike reflection of sunlight glancing off
The slick tapered length of one exquisite thigh
As the summer clouds above us broke for some interval
Not quite long enough to grasp yet brief enough to light
The whole & at last softly recuperated body

Of the singular living day

Memphis

Memphis

(EAP, d. 8/17/77?)

Sometimes when I'm bored by my own sins

I slip on my old falcon helmet
& drive the still glistening pink chariot
Beyond these lonely gates of grace

& down into a land the books call Memphis

Where the shadows of the pyramids
Still fall along Beale Street from a distance
Halfway around our once-and-future world

I fasten on the twin gold-plated Sun discs

To my helmet's stereo earplates
So I can listen to those tender sexual prayers
The King kindly left to us

& with the bass line pounding I push the horses

Of the Caddy up close to the raving red line & past
Until the trees themselves are screaming by
Oh Mother Isis Mother Gladys

I miss those days he'd shoot out the blank eyes

Of all those static gods around us saying
Now Horus just watch how the vapor of their minds
Blows through the room as delicately as night

& as he put down the .44

He'd start the low part of our gospel harmony
To *Swing low, sweet chariot, coming for to . . .*
& we'd fall apart laughing just the way we would

As boys off playing in the papyrus reeds waving

Along the riverbanks in spring . . .
& after I wrapped his cold body in silk windings
Then hid him beneath the earth of the temple grounds

I watched his *ka* fly suddenly everywhere its melody

Striking the leaves & long chords of sunlight
Until even the wood of his mandolins blistered
With tears of clear resin & the silent mockingbirds cried

Later I found the list of duties he'd left each of us

Open on that ebony grand piano exactly
Where his favorite hymnal should have been
To Ettore still in mourning in Milan he'd charged

With the perfection of the espresso pot & other

Privileged sacraments of the spirit's design
To his silky priestesses and devoted bodily servants
He'd left a catalogue of scandals to reveal at will

In order to make him seem more desperately human

& thereby to stage his eventual return to this world
As utterly miraculous   & to me of course
He left the holy hologram machine

The one no larger than a doctor's black bag

I carry with me everywhere so that when the time
Seems right to me I can raise his image *anywhere*
Anywhere at all in this world

Maybe in a restaurant or on a busy street corner

Or even across the tired eyelids of a hairdresser
As she bends above her first customer of the day
Suddenly jerking awake as she's consumed

By the lake of memory which is his love washing

Over her like the echo of his unforgivable voice
I do this for love as well as duty
I do this to remind them that their Osiris

Is never far from them & never beyond

The daily accident of their simplest devotions
This is my job the one he left for me
To keep a world so desperate for faith alive

With the single possibility & hope that his wild

Living sneer & wink
Will give us back the very things we still desire
Those bodies we once threw so recklessly away

The friends we sacrificed for other friends

The pulse of that voice accompanying each of us
The first time we did anything loving
That really mattered & might still once again

In the ever hushed & distant Memphis of our dreams

Fleurs Mystiques

The Unsayable, the Unknowable & You

Lately, only three things really interest me—
The unsayable, the unknowable & you.

The colors of the morning edge in a little
Here, as a backdrop to the towers of the Loire;

Ash white limbs languish above the river's muted reds,
Its blazing lace of late-summer's light, that

Holy figure. Around us—swirling—those grains of
Rumor, pearls of salt kissed from an open palm . . .

Each night suggests the fortunes of the moon,
The way our room remains requited by desire.

My prize: A night alone (again) with you, tracing
This brocade of sweat along your amber shoulder.

Let's weave together the dawn's superior light—
A script of bodies, inscribed by the summer's night.

Night

When Carole Laure stepped onto the black stage
At the Bobino, she got such a hand

That Lewis Furey, at the baby grand
Back in the shadows, had to grin. That image

Of her, singing in a single spotlight,
Hair rippling as she gave it a brief

Toss, just like in *Get Out Your Handkerchiefs,*
Made us feel the world would be all right.

Later, drinking Armagnac at Le Dôme,
Watching the late-night Easter week parade

Down Montparnasse, I thought I saw, in a jade
& mauve raincoat, Carole Laure—walking home

With Lewis Furey, in a group of friends . . .
All laughing, as if the night would never end.

Nervalesque

I am the shadow—the widower—the inconsolable,
The prince of Aquitaine at the ruined tower:
My only star is dead,—& my star-studded lute
Bears the black sun of melancholy.

In the night of the tomb, You who consoled me,
Give me back Posilipo & the sea of Italy,
The flower so pleasing to my desolate heart,
& the trellis where vines wove with the rose.

Am I Love or Phoebus? Lusignan or Biron?
My forehead is still red with the queen's kiss;
I've dreamt in the grotto where the siren swims . . .

& I've twice crossed the Acheron triumphantly,
Tuning, string by string, the lyre of Orpheus
To the sighs of the saint & the fairy's cries.

II. ANTEROS

You ask why I have so much rage in my heart
& on this supple neck, a wild untamed head;
It's because I'm descended from the line of Antaeus,
I can turn back arrows against the conquering god.

Yes, I'm one of those inspired by the Avenger;
He marked my brow with his curled lip;
Beneath the pallor of Abel, alas! bloody now,
Sometimes I have Cain's implacable blush!

Jehovah! the last, beaten by your genius,
Who, at the depths of hell, cried: "Tyranny!"
Was Belus my grandfather or my father Dagon . . .

They plunged me three times in the waters of Cocytus,
& alone protecting my Amalekite mother, I again
Sow at her feet the teeth of the ancient dragon.

III. Delfica

Do you know, Daphne, this old ballad,
At the foot of the sycamore, or beneath the white laurels,
Beneath the olive, the myrtle, or the trembling willows,
This song of love which always begins again? . . .

Do you recognize the TEMPLE with the huge peristyle,
& the bitter lemons inscribed by your teeth,
& that cave, fatal to imprudent guests,
Where the defeated dragon's ancient semen slept?

They'll come back, those Gods you still weep for!
Time will restore the order of past days;
The earth has trembled with a prophetic breath . . .

Yet the sibyl with the Latin face
Still sleeps beneath the arch of Constantine
—& nothing has disturbed that glowering portico.

Troubadour

I remember how my lover wept
That day I left the Academy of Troubadours
    & set out to prove myself & seek my fortune
Along the plains of Aquitaine, taking with me

    Only the rough clothing of my songs.
The rosewood face of my lute had been inlaid
    With carved ivory roses & exquisitely twined
Vines climbing the lute's sloping shoulders

    & up the long length of its polished neck.
My cloak was lined with a violet satin & even
    The wild Tartar angle of my cheekbones
Was something already gossiped about in the courts

    Of Pisa, Rome & Florence—
& as the valet brought my ancient Triumph TR3
    Up before the beachfront restaurant
Where we'd been sharing our somber final meal

    My lover slowly stroked my parted lips
With the hard, varnished backs of her fingernails—
    As if she were strumming her own ebony lap harp—
Saying to me as her glistening Mercedes appeared

So suddenly at the curb like some black
Stallion rising from the nearby waves, O sing well my child
    & remember every heart's a bit like mine, my dear,
Just a simple door thrown open by the lyre's prick . . .

Rhapsody

In the dictionary of sapphires
Only the rain confesses its regrets.
Even the Venetian courtier asleep
At the end of the bed forgets

The naked jewels at his fingertips.
Still, in our own prosaic silence
Even a simple breath upon the ear
Is a kind of violence.

Then, beyond the facets of sex,
Level as moonlight, some lost aspect
Of solitude touches your shoulders,
Still bare & glistening with sweat,

The soft white of new ice & fragile as air;
& so I know I must take care.

Fleurs Mystiques

In the dream he ran his fingers along
The perfectly matched grains of the parquet
Of the monk's quarters   as outside
The fields began erupting in false bouquets

The Siamese bells sounding in relay
From the sanded teak porch
Of the temple
                              & suddenly
A bird-of-paradise rose
In the green heat of the midnight as Jeanne

Kissed his pale erect & nervous nipple

& in a letter to his mother Baudelaire

Described in elaborate & exhaustive detail
Walking the derelict gardens
Of the abandoned Japanese consulate in Paris
The little wooden bridges all creaking

In disrepair   their blood red paint
Flaking in long sensual curls
& at the very back of the grounds below
An abject willow tree
He gazed into the black pond overgrown
With weeds & festering mosses
A wound run to gangrene yet somehow
Depthless as obsidian or ebony
& as he stared   no image
Was returned not even of his own lips
Parting like a lily's sneer not even of
Those preternatural cat-eyes of the future
Nothing simply nothing   only
That rippling pulse radiating from the locus
Of his own skull: its cathedral of terrible thirst
As he recalled the phrase Buddha
Had once told the kneeling monks beside the banyan
Was the emblem for all such simple suffering
As his: *the lotus kiss:::opiate time*

He was walking an especially unromantic street
A street rancid with debris & coal smoke
Yet a hand fell on his shoulder so lightly

He believed that a tiny Phoenix
Like a mimosa blossom
Had settled quietly beside his ear   perhaps

At his collarbone just before blazing up
In its resurrection of flame & it spoke
The very words he'd heard Jeanne

Say to him that morning as
She rose on one elbow in the wrecked bed
Do not forgive reality   Charles   it will

Never forgive you

He had stepped beyond the canvas of his life

& this had been far more difficult
Than any of the mystic manuals had first
Led him to believe   yet
At that moment as he passed from the frame of light

Into the black pane of the other world

& although around him he could see nothing
But the surging waves of obsidian fog
He could smell that blossoming of Jeanne's body
The familiar fragrance of sex that would arise

& fill the entire landscape of his moon-pocked soul

Night after night after night
As he rubbed her hips with the cool rank oils
Of the night-blooming star jasmine

& the powders of ruby myrrh

I'm sorry he'd said to his mother & stepfather
This evening even I seem to have exhausted

All of my moral platitudes

He stood at the altar of absolute light

Holding up a priceless Renaissance lute
Carved of rosewood & maple
Its mouth a necklace of precisely tooled roses

Their petals trembling & blackening slightly
At their edges as he sang
& every song recalled those rows of fallen arbors

Framing another lost   hellish note of the sublime

Jeanne dreamt of the hollow shadow of St. Francis
Frozen in the riotous petals of stained glass

Of a single cold petal pressed in the monk's damp hand

As he himself dreamt he'd been kissing the soft
Forgiveness of Jeanne's open palms

Each of her fingers burning like a courtesan's

Long taper with a final sexual flame
Her flickering white nails lighting their way

Through the collapsed & blackened accordion hallways

No   Jeanne had said   *No*   *please*
              Never forgive them

The Red Leaves of Night

Chevalier d'Or

Sometimes not even behind his back

His old friends called him the *chevalier d'or*
Not in kindness nor even humor but envy

& each morning as he stepped

From the ancient porcelain tub onto the freezing
Ochre & maroon Mexican tiles of the bathroom floor

He could see in the mist-veiled mirror

That hard wet helmet of golden hair
He'd worn for years like an aging French rock star

Yet at certain moments on particular evenings

When the light in some desolate nightclub in Nice
Fell just right a woman who was a stranger

Might say to him how much he reminded her

Of Johnny Hallyday & then his lips would glisten
In the smoky air & his eyes

Would blink their eloquent sadness into song

& everywhere in the world weary companionable women
Would arise & touch again the soft lute of their

Most ancient & trusted troubadour

Water Serpents

Beneath the lit silk of your naked body

When you move your bones move like nervous water snakes
A complicated Medusan nest of rippling eels

Currents in the dawn river

My own body littered by broken limbs of almond sunlight
As your breath uncoils its music & anxious histories of sexual
   pride

Echo from the hotel room next door

As our own pasts rise through the water like sacred filaments
& in our dead lovers' eyes we can recall

Woman upon woman upon man swirling in a pool of
   memorylessness

& upon the shore the day arrives entwined in its sisterly mass of
   red hair
Those brash & roiling fields of ruby kelp where

The dark sailor's body is found

Portrait

There is in his daughter's gaze
A solemnity so elegant
It must seem to some
The very definition of love

Though her profile guards
Any true window to emotion
Any genuine reflection of
Her understanding of her father's

Objective protective despair
As her beauty is shielded
By white & her lips in their easy
Parting draw back

From any kiss now
She is watching in the distance
Of the chapel a whole narrative
Beginning to assemble

One which finds the breath
Of the huge organ an unholy
Accompaniment its
Bellows moaning heavily over

What just a moment ago
The virginal & clear morning
Had promised to unveil forever
Yet which (now) the white day

Seems so certain to withhold

Patience

Patience is in my clothes
She said to me at the evening's end
But never in my heart
Never in my arms or thighs & so

As I look at you she said
I wonder how I've spent even
One night with you let alone
So many years & I suppose

She said that loathing is
Too strong a word since what
I feel now is so much closer
To contempt & pity both

That it's become wearying even
To watch you pour the wine
& so depressing to feel
The draft of the night as you

Open a window onto the starlight
You believe she said will make me
Love you as you once believed I loved you
Though of course she said that's

Simply what I said

Accomplishment

Touch me here just below
The nipple where I cannot see

Use the mirror of your lips
Touch me here where the faintest skin awakens

As you lift those leaves of moonlight from my shoulders
Touch me here where my legs fall open

Touch me here beyond the frail breastbone
That place complicated & caged by Eve's own ribs

Those many discards of God's twisted lattice
His cool marimba of borrowed bone

Touch me here again where what bleeds begins

Naked

He'd left the screening room
Groggy & somewhat depressed

Wondering how many sleepless nights
Were left before he'd finish

The Maestro's biography
& the catalogue of those rare raw films

The Maestro had left unedited in cans
In the attic study of a derelict Nantucket home

So he walked abstractedly
To the Museum of Natural History

& strolled his favorite corridors—the gem
& mineral collections where the dark

Was blasted by the jeweled light
Ice green fingers of tourmaline

Garnets & peridots & jade all
A kind of crystalline punctuation

& as he stood before the nipples of rose
Quartz he could in fact taste the ease

Of such opulence reflecting the way
Even God trusts that the light of stone arises

Most beautifully uncut

Ravenesque

I dreamt a golden snake
Unravelled like an ancient scroll along your arm
Scales of parchment or papyrus
Riding the swirling light as

They fell slowly to the slate islands
Of the cold floor
Where I lay barely awake
Looking up into a face framed by

The black corona of your hair so
Ravenesque & flaked by coins of golden
Documents all of which no doubt
Held the meaning of your distant gaze

Your eyelids themselves slowly closing
At last when after a time
The robe of reeds you wore draped
Across your shoulders parted

As your arms parted
& the snake lifted its head of beaten gold
Your bare breasts slowly lifting
Toward the sudden light of the heavens

Which was the unbroken surrender of God

The Pianist

In the apartment next door
The new tenant's playing
His piano again this morning
Just at dawn

It is the dazzling ancient Bechstein
I watched the movers hoist up
From the street into the open double
Windows of that familiar living room

A room I'd once spent hours in holding
A glass of wine or listening
To your stories of a Viennese childhood
Where now you've returned to forever

Hold a few final sheets of music
Like crumpled earth between your hands
& every time that somber man next door
Plays those lieder you loved I swear

A woman's unholy voice dusts the morning air

Not a Man

I am not a man who generally
Loves the grace of summer quiet

I prefer the sneer of winter
& the grit of ash smeared upon the air

But when you stood on the veranda
Of the old farmhouse as the night breezes played

Over the folded pleats of that snowy nightgown
I could believe the heavenly owl

Crying in the distance was only moments away
From his desperate descent & sublime happiness

Opening his wings above that silver streak of purpose
Moonlight had swollen into a special prey

Stories

She told me only three stories
In the week before she died

The first about the child she'd lost
A boy just seven

A climbing accident that summer
She'd taken a cabin in the Pyrenees

& the second was not a story at all
But simply a description of the Alfa Romeo

Her husband's lover drove up
To the door of their house the day he left her

It was the color she said of a mustard field
& then she turned to me & held out a snapshot

She'd taken from the drawer of her bedside table
A photo of herself on an empty pier at twenty

Nude she recalled beneath her robe of copper orchids
Which required she insisted no explanation but instead

As she required of me just this song of simple mystery

Levels of Retreat

It was a good city in which to hide
The lake lapped quietly
At the feet of every hotel & the swans
At the mercy of the seasons

Had at last returned
To zigzag along its shores
& we felt inviolate chaste & drunk
With the ease of circumstance

Lost in the open pages of our escape
& the city itself rose up the hillside
In its blocks of stone & hewn timbers
Painted yellow & the faintest pink

Ascending to the pale medieval chapel
That presided above the water & its
Reflected quiet
Don't worry reckless strangers don't

Think twice before shedding your silences
With your passports & your coats
Like lambs in the hands of Michelangelo
Nothing can hurt you here

Apple Orchard

In the apple orchard she sat on a small wood bench
Placed almost exactly at the center of the grove
For moments like these when it was important to stop the world

& let everything else pass by even the wind with its scent of sweet
    rots
& the snowflake petals of the lush apple trees falling around her
But of course as she stood she grew dizzy with the applause of

The paper-faced red poppies at her feet their bleeding laughter
& frank open gazes so shocking to someone so used to the
    ordinary guile
Of friends & when at last her composure returned it was as if a
    snake

Had uncoiled within her & she cupped the perfect globe of lust
    in her hand

Waves

After the disenchantment
Comes the despair he'd warned
& so not being one to ignore
A friend's advice

I took the mail boat
Out to the island where
He said he'd once spent
An important summer of

His life retching out
His guts every morning after
A hopeless affair
During which he'd learned

He had no capacity to wound
Those who had done
Nothing except to desire what
He too relentlessly desired that is

Up to that moment his rival
Which is to say the husband
Of his lover covered
The gunmetal walls of a bedroom

With an abstract of bloody waves

What He Said

My friend said to me
The one thing I'd never do
Is to sleep with another man's
Wife no actually he didn't say

"Another man's" he said instead
"A friend's" meaning I supposed me
& though this was many years ago
& meant I know

To be reassuring I couldn't help
But think Methinks he doth et cetera
& as the sunlight this morning lifted
These gold ribbons of smoke into the air

I began once again to remember
The dulled gilt mirror of the vanity
Where one night she sat in her peach
Gown long after I'd gone to bed

& beside her the small white telephone
Which he could now no longer at last
I understood from the distance of these years
—No longer & for whatever reason—

Make ring for her late into the solitary night

Mystic Eyes

It was the opiate chartreuse
Of her aura my friend the twice-failed mystic
First pointed out to me one evening

As Lara lifted her head in the dead-pale moonlight
Of the summer's pause

We'd all been talking out on the patio
Of polished flagstones in the high & crisp New Mexico air
& I had to confess I'd come to the end of something

Though the simplicity of what she'd needed from me
Still held us as closely as the vast impossibility
Of what I'd asked of her

Which made it of course the very definition of love

Meaning I suppose a sexual wound tempered in that chilling well
Of the bitter & clearly ordinary world

Two

At different times in my life I'd adored them both

& so when they found themselves in love
Who else for consolation & advice should they turn to

Though Lara was in her Chinese phase & the dark blood walls

Of her bedroom gave Solange pause she admitted
Though the low black-enameled bed signified to her every luxury

She'd never had & I suppose I envied Lara waking

To the fawn-colored robes that would drape then fall from
    Solange's
Shoulders in the smoky edge of the evening though

Lara herself I remember preferred to walk through the house

Completely naked at any hour with a bearing that might be
Envied by both London bankers & deposed island queens
    though it

Terrified her gardeners & cleaning lady—that resolute fierceness
    in her stride

& the erect pride of her scarlet nipples & the wild fox blaze of
    pubic hair
Lighting her way all of these many years from one long-blessed

Grace unto another

Red Wheat: Montana

There is a kind of weeping so inconsolable
It occasions only silence

Just as there is a kind of silence so horrible it requires weeping

Naked at the tall bedroom mirror she had shorn in piles
The magnificent red hair I had always loved

The blanket of curls I would pull over my body at night

A ragged field of red wheat clipped & bundled at harvest
& as I stood in the doorway she turned & said

Next week they said next week the treatments will "commence"

& in that pause I saw the sneer of a smile begin
As she said but today you & I will go & introduce ourselves

At Madame Récamier's Modern House of Wigs

Water Serpents (II)

When they found her daughter in the river

She stood at the muddy folds of the bank with her fists
Shoved deep into the soft wool pockets of the black pea coat

Pockets that had somehow molded themselves around her hands
& as they lifted the girl's bare body up out of the eelgrass & reeds

A faint golden sheen of oil rippled along the skin like a glove of
    fish scales

& then the twisted corpse was laid out along the blue police
    blanket
& the near & distant sirens reddened the water & the nails of rain

& everywhere inside her a gallery of faces clenched against her
    given name

The Bowl

The world as a goldfish bowl remains
The lesson we must learn unerringly
He said before we understand the ways
The lens of searing unrelenting

Regard will be held up against
Our every breath & make
Ridiculous every pretense
Of defense

& rumor is the true pornography
Of a life   the love of the voyeur
For what he himself can never
Bring himself or come to

Or herself as it goes around
Quite democratically this disease
Which is a hatred for one's instincts
For the world & its quite erring flesh

(Its weary flesh) each touch
Reduced by the watcher's gaze
Into some petrified gesture
Of panic

The way the water itself swirls
As the child reaches within
& lifts the twisting golden body
From the stilled globe of its own

Clarified eye

Music

It became my passion to explain everything
With music even the randomness of starlight or death

I was convinced I could find their formulas & chant

The course of my reasoning to the assembled Academy
In the melodies & harmonies I had begun to hear

At every moment issuing from my body

Sometimes a tune so innocent & simple
Flocks of sleeping sheep rose & left their shepherds

Sometimes a passage so ecstatic even Mozart's father

Left his calling card in the silver bowl by the door
& every sphinx of confusion I'd dragged with me

Into this concert of the death's-head spheres

Parted its heavy lips & whispered to me secrets
So rare & hollow they left me at last with nothing to live for

& no songs left to sing

Lecture

The frankness of the gaze is disconcerting I'm afraid
He told the class in his lecture on the odalisque
& after he'd finished his cleverly banal & patronizing talk
He'd watched the students slowly file out like bored convicts
Up the long slope of the theaterlike classroom
Except for the one who knew he
Knew that he was completely full of shit
The way she stood at the doorway looking down at him
With her feet spread & her hips locked & pivoted clearly
Toward some future beyond him
                          Her head perfectly erect her hair
Pulsing obsidian in the fluorescent glare
Her gaze saying not the "Fuck me" he had supposed of the
    painting
But instead a fine & resolute "Fuck you"

Prayer to Ondine

To live with you Ondine
I have given up the air of summer
I have spread my body like a star's
& I have foresworn the morning light

To live with you Ondine
I have wrapped my shoulders in a shawl
Of charred coral & built at the sea's edge
A cathedral of white driftwood

To live with you Ondine
I would give myself to any of your sisters
All you need to do is ask
Even the blue sister who is your dead twin

To live with you Ondine
I will be the green subject of your hunger
The brutal window where a face shatters in the wind
To live with you Ondine I would let the sad lost waves

Lick the wicked salt from my bones

Adam

It's ridiculous to confess
Such a superficial thing
Yet it's true I was first stunned
By the extraordinary whiteness

Of her skin a chalked mannequin so
Pale & translucent her hair seemed
A blond halo of almost shadowlike
Depth & the red glow of her mouth

Was like the distant smudge of
A stoplight pulsing in the dawn fog
& I was completely shaken & taken
As she lay back against

The leopard print shawl she'd draped
Over the chaise in her studio just before
She'd slowly undressed the way the sky
Sweeps itself free of random clouds

So what did you expect of me
To pretend I was a far more serious man
With fierce philosophical complaints
To protect me from my own rash hungers

Or did you know all along I was in love

A Naked Truth

If you cannot please everyone with
your deeds or your art, please a few.
To please many is bad.
                    —Schiller

It is the mirror
In which art itself sees
Itself reflected the way
A lover sees the world

Reflected in her own lover's
Eyes just as it is
The reflected gaze of art
That suffocates the coiling

Rumors & the bared lips
At the closed door that hunger
Of envy that desperate impulse
Of the lie

How long can the hope
Of pleasing those for whom
Pleasure is terror seem
Even a casual ideal

When the warm body
Of truth presses the facts of
Its flesh against you
How else do the brush & the pen

The marble page & the scored staff
All fade from the mind's
Dark & gather
With the day's simple light

The streaming hair of sunrise
Reddening the mirror of
The mountain lake
Where the only truth left ripples

Like a body silently & nakedly
& ecstatically as art

Beeches

The forest is its own thanksgiving
Walking a mile or so from the road
Past the lake & ancient post office
I skim the long bodies of the beech trees

The elegant ascension of their slender trunks
A kind of gorgeous illusory play
Of white bars against the dark ochre matting
Of the earth below

Peace is where you find it
As here the last secret of the dawn air mixes
With a nostalgia so perfumed by misery
Only the rhythm of the walk itself

Carries me beyond the past
To say I miss you is to say almost nothing
To say the forest is the sanctuary of ghosts
Is only the first step of my own giving way—

Not the giving up—just the old giving thanks

The Park

It was I think in a small town in Ohio

I taped to the wall above my office desk the postcard
Of Klimt's painting called *The Park*

An example of cliché so profuse it touched my heart

Consoling me each time I turned my glance to its
Storm of tiny moth-sized leaves shimmering over all but the
    bottom

Ribbon of the canvas where the rows of the trunks individuate

The mass of the pulsing foliage above
A figure in a kimono or a robe so lush it too seems foliate

Stands apart from two other figures similarly dressed

But (the two) huddled closely together & moving off the sheer
Right edge of the canvas

& the solitary figure remains oddly hesitant & indistinct

& pensive although
Perhaps she is simply realizing that she does not wish to go

Where all of the others wish to go

Solitude

My life is gypsy solitude
Riotous aloneness travelling
The patched groves of misunderstanding
—Ah to be a circus unto oneself

You said once is to give away
Everything each evening to that crowd
Of lovers just as working forever
City to city is to be always the stranger

Others choose to wake beside
So forget the last ghosts of the mist
Hanging like a sexual musk
Forget the dangling silk scarves on

Flamenco dancers' bedposts
Put your heels to my shoulders
Or to the road or to the echoing
Polished wood of the small dance floor

Those rippling machine-gun guitars
Stuttering every apology you will forget
To make until it is too late & you
Become again as obscure as the delicate

Lantern disappearing into the gathering rain

An Invitation

Let me invite you to kiss
The smirk of the Medusa
Reach to touch the victory still
Naked in my hand   it is

So brutal an understanding
I will demand of you in your weakness
So attendant an inscription to
A century's failure

If every hundred years a certain
Style evolves out of mystery into mystery
Then perhaps this evening was meant
To be a clever clue & if what matters

To you is not the disconsolate
Reportage of your sisters & brothers
But the unheard songs slowly swelling
At the horizon's edge

As the girl with the ivory flute
Unravels the trance of summer blossoms along
The wind then here Sister Warrior is where
I'll stand beside you: at the broken wall

Of that fortress where lips of ice have sinned

The Red Leaves of Night

In my dream we are walking together

Through a forest of blanched birch & ragged beech perhaps
I know only that the trunks reflect their mottled

& luminous white bodies in the moonlight

& as we walk to some destination we seem not to know
I notice that the forest floor is matted again

With a blanket of fallen red leaves each as narrow as a finger

Thin pages torn from a pilgrim's book & some
Seem to have scrawled upon them sentences that themselves

Are written in the sticky red of blood entries

In the journal I heard you promise God you will burn tomorrow
& as we walk I can feel beneath my bare feet how soft

& cushioned by such fallenness this passage has become

This journey through the forest of the night
Along a path of red sorrows leading us together to some newly
    solitary

& distant home

About the Author

Over the course of his career David St. John has been honored with many of the most significant prizes for poets, including fellowships from the National Endowment for the Arts and the John Simon Guggenheim Memorial Foundation, the Prix de Rome Fellowship in Literature from the American Academy and Institute of Arts and Letters, and a grant from the Ingram Merrill Foundation. His work has been published in countless literary magazines, including *The New Yorker, The Paris Review, Poetry, American Poetry Review, Antaeus, Harper's,* and *The New Republic,* and has been widely anthologized. He has taught creative writing at Oberlin College and Johns Hopkins University and currently teaches at the University of Southern California.